Sleep Tight Tonight

A Play

Michael Snelgrove

Samuel French – London
New York – Sydney – Toronto – Hollywood

CHARACTERS

Dr Max Housden
Operator 1
Operator 2
Operator 3
Operator 4
Minister
Dr Leppard
Coley
Amanda Thain
Margaret
American Ambassadress
American General
Cameron
Interviewer
TV Technicians
TV Floor Manager
Man
Woman
Man
Mrs Judd
Young Woman
Villagers
Police Superintendent
Police Officers
Bishop
Reverend Blishen

SLEEP TIGHT TONIGHT*

The public bar of a rather seedy inner-city pub. The furniture is motley, with perhaps a space invaders or pinball machine, and there is a general atmosphere that stops just short of sawdust on the floor

The Lights come up on Max, forty to fiftyish and magnificently untidy, at the bar ordering a drink—a large one! He moves away to sit at a table but instead comes downstage to talk to the audience. Other men and women, also in the bar area, assume various roles throughout the action

Max It started like this . . .

The lighting changes to a red effect on a control room of some sort—flashing lights, warning buzzers, all very discreet and low key. Various Operators watch screens—the light reflected on their faces

Operator 1 What's going on?
Operator 2 A marginal decay in orbit.
Operator 1 How marginal is marginal?
Operator 2 Currently two point eight per cent—but worsening.
Operator 1 What's the safety parameter on this one?
Operator 3 Delay of six point two per cent and we've lost it.
Operator 1 Call the Director.
Operator 2 Three point five per cent increasing.
Operator 4 Can't we give it a squirt?
Operator 1 That's not my decision.
Operator 2 Four point two per cent.
Operator 1 What's caused this?
Operator 4 Could be a collision of some sort. Meteor or old satellite.
Operator 1 Missile?
Operator 4 Don't be paranoid.
Operator 2 Five point six per cent.

---

* N.B. Paragraph 3 on page ii of this Acting Edition regarding photo-copying and video-recording should be carefully read.

Operator 1 Compute that.
Operator 3 The retros couldn't push it back now.
Operator 1 Not even with a prolonged squirt?
Operator 3 Not even with a Saturn Five stuffed up its backside.
Operator 1 Where's the Director?
Operator 4 Dinner party, I think.
Operator 1 Get him.
Operator 4 They're trying.
Operator 2 Five point nine per cent.

Silence

Six point two per cent.

The phone rings

Operator 4 It's the Director. Apparently they've only just reached the Stilton.

The Lights come up on the bar as normal. Max goes and sits at a table

Max I never drink. (*He looks at his glass*) I rarely drink. I actually don't enjoy it. I don't like the taste but tonight I'm after the effect of it because I have to fly and I hate flying. Whenever I fly, I have to get pissed—drunk, sorry. I never use rude words—unless I'm pissed. Come to think of it I hate the effect of getting drunk as well but ... Time to explain. Explanation time. Max Housden, how do you do, nice to meet you, etc. etc. I'm an astro-physicist and a bit of an engineer and I'm reckoned to be pretty hot; and I wouldn't say that if I hadn't drunk this. The point is that at the moment my head is so full. There's this continuous stream of pictures running round and round in my head—like a film loop, and I suppose that's confusing me because normally everything is so sharp and precise and well laid out in there. I'm a scientist after all, and the training pays off—but not tonight. Tonight I've got an uneasy feeling that what's going on in there is a story of some description that's struggling to be told. Which is also very surprising because usually I don't go in for stories much. I don't usually go in for anything much—except astro-physics and a bit of engineering. It more and more seems to me that I've dedicated everything to an ideal which is all very well until ... I'll tell you the story. It

won't be the full story, and some of it will be guesswork because
we shit-hot astro-physicists can't be everywhere at once, but I do
have an imagination—that's another thing that has come as a
surprise to me recently—and it's more than likely that some of
this story will be a bit confused, a bit hazy. Clouded by this
stuff, most probably, so please make allowances. I am also tired.
I haven't been sleeping. I'd like nothing more than to sleep
properly. Scene One.

*The lighting changes and the people at the bar group themselves for a
scene*

Just a moment.

The lighting changes back

It's very hard explaining what's going on in your head—I can't
just sit here and tell you the story—I'd get confused and might
even fall asleep. So, I'll use these people to show you. Just
ordinary people in a pub. They'll still be ordinary people in a
pub, having a drink, meeting friends, whatever. But what they
don't know is they're in my head telling my story. They are an
externalization of my imagination if you will. Objective correla-
tives—that's a literary phrase I picked up somewhere, God
knows where. Scene One.

*The lighting changes to the entrance hall of a large house. The
doorbell rings, the knocker is knocked. The hall light is turned on.
The Minister appears, rumpled in his dressing-gown. He is between
forty and fifty. He opens the door to discover Leppard, fortyish, well
dressed in a dinner suit*

Minister Yaagh?

Leppard Minister?

Minister Whargh?

Leppard I'm so sorry to have to disturb you at this ghastly hour,
but what I have to say couldn't be divulged over the phone, even
one as scrambled as a plate of eggs.

Minister What are you talking about?

Leppard Might I come in? I seem to be over dressed. I do
apologize. I was called away from a dinner party I'm afraid.
Before the Stilton too. (*He comes in*) Thank you.

Minister What is it, Leppard? I'd just got off.

Leppard ORSONE, Minister.

Minister Whorson?

Leppard ORSONE, Minister. The Orbiting Research Station Over Northern Europe. These scientists and their acronyms.

Minister What about ORSONE?

Leppard It's coming down.

Minister Coming down? But it's only just gone up.

Leppard It is unfortunate, I agree.

Minister When you say coming down, you mean . . .

Leppard Crashing—yes. Crashing back to earth with some volition. Perhaps they should have called it ICARUS.

Minister Is this confirmed?

Leppard I'm afraid so. We received confirmation from Easter Island half an hour ago.

Minister Easter Island?

Leppard It's where we keep our tracking station. As I remember, you visited it with a parliamentary delegation last year. I saw a photograph of you posed in front of one of those extraordinary statues they have down there. You were wearing an Hawaiian shirt—and sort of grass skirt. It excited considerable comment in *The Daily Telegraph* at the time.

Minister It can't be coming down. Not already.

Leppard Well you know what they say.

Minister No I don't.

Leppard That was goes up . . .

Minister Are you being flippant?

Leppard It's a proverb.

Minister I know its a proverb! I recognize a proverb when I see one, thank you very much. Where's it coming down?

Leppard There you have me by the hip, Minister.

Minister What?

Leppard There—as they say—is the rub.

Minister Who is this "they" they keep on about?

Leppard To be frank, we don't as yet know where it will come down.

Minister Then you'd better find out, hadn't you?

Leppard I'll put Max Housden on it. He's our best man. He can do some feasability studies.

Minister It'll come down in Australia—or some other godforsaken place, won't it? These things always do. The Australian outback.

Leppard It's a little more complicated than that.

Minister I don't like complications.

Leppard If you remember ORSONE is a Pan-European Technological Venture?

Minister Yes, yes.

Leppard Which means we built it with several of our European
friends.

Minister I'm not a mental defective, Leppard.

Leppard Of course not, Minister. You will remember the Americans took it up for us in the Shuttle. The complication is in the
fact that, in return for putting ORSONE into orbit for us—our
friends across the pond asked a small favour in return.

Minister Oh my God.

Leppard I see you remember what that favour was.

Minister I do.

Leppard If the . . . payload that they put into ORSONE were to
. . . misbehave on impact or re-entry it could be potentially very
embarrassing . . .

Minister This is disastrous.

Leppard It's certainly rather tricky.

Minister Can you get your people together tomorrow? Nine
o'clock?

Leppard Of course.

Minister Your best people.

Leppard I'll put Housden in charge.

Minister I've met Housden, haven't I? I remember him. Brilliant
scientist.

Leppard How could you possibly tell that?

Minister He had custard all down his pullover.

The Lights cross fade to the bar. Max has another drink

Max At least, that's how I imagined it. I might have embellished it
a little—but there we are that's imagination for you. An
unpredictable factor. Up until now, the only imagination I've
experienced is of the scientific kind, the logical kind—you know
the kind of thing. If proposition A works, then conceivably that
proposition plus proposition B will take it one stage further
towards result C. A plodding imagination proceeding step by
step using trial and error to its logical conclusion; an imagination that's always been connected with abstract propositions;
with figures; statistics; machines. Never, until now, with people.

ORSONE was the result of that imagination. ORSONE was my brain child if you like, or, at least, the nearest to a child I am ever likely to get. I gave birth to ORSONE and I dedicated my life to bringing it up and nuturing it. Quite pathetic really. Scene Two. This one's pure fact. I was there . . .

The Lights come up on a table arranged as for a meeting. The Minister presides. Also present are Leppard, Coley (a representative from the American Embassy) and Amanda Thain, a very efficient PR lady

Minister Where's Housden?

Leppard He was informed of the meeting Minister—but you know what these scientists are.

Minister I thought you were a scientist?

Leppard Alas. Bureaucracy has long since ursuped the place of science in my capacity as Director.

Coley That's very well put, Dr Leppard.

Leppard Thank you.

Max enters the meeting

Max Sorry. I was side-tracked. Something from the computer.

Minister You're here anyway so let's get the introductions over. This is Max Housden, principal scientific officer on the ORSONE project. Mr Coley from the American Embassy. Miss Thain—Dep. of Inf.

Max Sorry?

Minister Department of Information.

Max Ah.

Minister And, of course, you know Leppard. Now then, I won't waste time because I don't believe we have much time to waste. ORSONE is coming down and that is a fact. A regrettable fact but a fact nevertheless. The purpose of this small working party is to oversee the course of Operation Icarus—as I have chosen to call it.

Leppard clears his throat

And to make this unfortunate incident as palatable as we possibly can. Now it seems to me that we have three main areas of concern. (a) To establish precisely where the thing will come down.

Max Thing?

(b) To liaise with the Government, or governments, involved and (c) to present the whole thing to the public in as decent a light as is possible. Now then, Leppard, perhaps you can fill us in on the first point?

Leppard Max? Max?

Max Sorry, I was miles away.

Leppard We'd appreciate your full attention.

Max I was just thinking that it is a long time since I thought of ORSONE as a thing. I think of it as almost human now.

Leppard Very touching. But can we persuade you to bend your mind around the appalling fact that this thing, all eight hundred tons of it, is going to come down somewhere and we'd rather like to have some idea where?

Max All the available data is being run through the computer now.

Leppard When can we expect an answer?

Max There's a lot of data.

Minister This evening?

Max It's a complicated program—very complicated.

Leppard Tomorrow?

Max Tomorrow—possibly.

Coley Do we have a time-frame as yet?

Max Sorry? A——?

Leppard An itinerary. Do we know when it will come down?

Max Oh yes.

Silence

Minister And?

Max About a week.

Minister About a week ...

Max Hard to be precise. Depends on the rate of orbit decay. What's an American doing here?

Amanda I thought these things burnt up when they hit the atmosphere?

Max They do.

Amanda So, what's the problem?

Max Usually.

Amanda Ah ...

Max But in this case our masters—who shall be nameless—thought it might be a good idea, in the interests of economy, to fit ORSONE with a form of protective heat shield, so that should we ever wish to get it down, we could put it back up again, thus saving money; hence it won't burn up all that much—if at all. It'll become white hot, of course, but won't actually burn up.

Amanda And if you can bring it down?

Max Again, in the interests of economy, those in power, who shall be nameless, wanted it launched at the first possible opportunity before we had properly calculated the means by which we could induce a controlled return to earth; the reasoning was that we could do that once it was up there. The result is that it's coming down but we can't control it—at least not with any degree of accuracy.

Minister We are not here to rake up the past, we are here to decide what can be done now.

Max And nobody's answered my question. What's an American doing here?

Leppard Yes. Well. Mr Coley is here, to—represent the interests of his country.

Max His country doesn't have an interest—except that they put ORSONE up there for us.

Leppard Precisely. But there are, shall we say, parts of the overall picture of which you are not aware.

Max What you mean is you haven't told me everything!

Minister Perhaps Mr Coley could . . .

Coley Thank you, Minister. I trust that everybody here . . .

Minister Has the highest security clearance—naturally.

Coley How much background do I need to fill in here?

Leppard We're all aware and grateful for your Government's invaluable contribution to the ORSONE project.

Coley It was an honour to be able to help such a worthwhile and meaningful mission, Dr Leppard, and it is our firm belief that this co-operation has strengthened the very special relationship that exists between our nations and those of——

Max Is this a private back-slapping or can anyone join in?

Minister Keep a civil tongue in your head, Housden.

Coley I stress the word co-operation, which implies a two-way process. As I think the Minister and Dr Leppard are aware, in return for putting ORSONE into orbit for our European friends, we were, in return, granted certain facilities . . .

Max Facilities?

Leppard Max . . .

Max What facilities?

Coley I thought Dr Housden would have been informed of this.

Leppard I thought it best not—in the circumstances.

Max What facilities?

Coley We were allowed to put on board certain—experiments of our own.

Max Of what nature?

Coley I believe our research department was very keen to see what effect prolonged orbit in space would have upon certain atomic properties.

Pause

Max You put nuclear devices on ORSONE?

Coley Really very small—nothing to speak of.

Max Warheads?

Coley Two—or so I believe. As I say, very small, one megaton each.

Max And you knew about this? About turning ORSONE into an orbiting weapon platform?

Leppard Of course.

Max And you let it go ahead?

Leppard We had a price to pay—this seemed the best way to pay for it.

Minister Naturally the Government fully supported Dr Leppard in this.

Max I'll bet.

Minister The decision was taken at full Cabinet level.

Max I can't tell you how reassured I feel about that.

Leppard I had hoped you'd take it rather better than this.

Max Does anybody know the effect of re-entry and impact on these things?

Coley Naturally, our people have thought about it very carefully.

Max And?

Coley One of two contingencies could occur. Firstly——

Max They'll go off. Or secondly—they won't. Correct?

Coley Loosely.

Leppard That's why it is of the utmost importance that we know where it's to come down, Max.

Minister I've told Leppard that I'm putting my money on Australia. Somewhere harmless like that. Yes. Perhaps we might turn
to point (c) on the agenda. To wit—the presentation of the
matters to the general public—which is where Miss Thain comes
in. Miss Thain is the Director of the Public Relations Department at the Dep. of Inf.—she is, I believe a leading expert in
these matters. Miss Thain . . .

Amanda Thank you, Minister. I think the essence of the problem
here is an image one. If we are not very careful in the way that
this whole problem is presented to the public, it could look as
though the whole incident is one long chapter of mis-manage-
ment and incompetence.

Max I see. We mustn't tell them the truth at any cost you mean?

Leppard This involves you too, Max—don't forget that.

Max Scientifically there is, nor was, nothing wrong with
ORSONE. If you hadn't allowed him and his lot to mess around
with payloads, if the Duty Controller had squirted it out into
space before orbit decay became critical. If the Director had
been there to make decisions——

Minister That'll do, Housden.

Max Don't blame science. The science is flawless.

Amanda Could I continue?

Minister Please do.

Amanda I think we must go out of our way to present the episode
to the public in as positive a manner as possible.

Max Positive—what do we say? Terribly sorry but there's a
chance of eight hundred tons of white hot metal coming down in
somebody's backyard and a possibility of a couple of nuclear
explosions, but don't worry just think positively about the
whole thing while you and your family are being fried to death.

Coley The other alternative, of course, is to operate on a "Need to
know" basis.

Minister Meaning?

Coley We resolve to find ourselves in a covert situation.

Max Meaning we don't tell anybody?

Coley Until we have to.

Leppard I hate to differ with any of our American cousins but I
think people might notice. Unless we tell them that it's just
another bit that's fallen off an airliner. That often happens.

Max Why not go the whole hog and tell them it's a gigantic bird's dropping? Listen, there are tracking stations all over the world who are eventually going to notice it dropping out of orbit. We'll have schoolboys with telescopes and crystal sets picking it up. It's that obvious.

Amanda By positive reinforcement I mean that we tell the public what a tremendous technological achievement ORSONE was; how it reflected European co-operation and has done so much to further our understanding not only of the scientific matter involved but of each other as fellow Europeans.

Max As an expression of the European ideal something falling flat on its face at seventeen thousand miles an hour certainly seems an appropriate metaphor.

Amanda To which end I think we have to think very carefully about the public face that presents this news. With respect, Minister, people don't entirely trust politicians any more, and I think the Falklands' crisis taught us a lot about the quality of Ministry spokesmen.

Minister What are you suggesting?

Amanda That we go for integrity. We go for a face that the public can trust and identify with; somebody who knows what he is talking about and who is intimately connected with the whole project, who can put a recognizable human face on the whole thing.

Max No.

Amanda You're already a fairly familiar face on television, Dr Housden.

Max I've been on the news a mere couple of times.

Leppard Picking up prestigious scientific awards. People like that.

Minister And those documentaries you appeared on, they went down very well—my wife enjoyed those.

Max No.

Leppard All we are asking for is a few interviews in which you can outline the scientific facts involved in the matter.

Max Including the warheads?

Amanda Ah. That would have to be handled very carefully.

Minister No point in mentioning that aspect until we know where it's going to come down.

Max One interview. Can I go now?

Minister Of course. We'd like those calculations as soon as you can. Time is of the essence.

Max Really? I thought your sort had nice safe bunkers to go to?

Max leaves the meeting

Minister Bit impertinent for my taste.
Leppard He's upset. He's spent about fifteen years on this. His colleagues call it his baby.
Minister Is this interview going to be embarrassing?
Amanda It'll be fine.
Minister Egg yolk this time I notice.
Leppard I beg your pardon, Minister?
Minister Egg yolk—down his tie.

They look at each other. The Lights cross fade to the bar where life goes on as usual

Max Impossible to say how I felt. All the easy words came to mind: disillusioned, used, abused, dirty; the banal vocabulary of betrayal. Imagine, if you can, leaving the woman you love most in the whole world alone in the room and returning find her with your best friend doing the filthiest thing you could possibly think of—and you'll have some idea of what I felt then. Scene Three. ORSONE Control Cafeteria.

The pub becomes the canteen restaurant of Control Centre—Max goes up to the service bar

Black coffee.

Leppard enters the canteen restaurant

Leppard That seemed to go quite well I thought. Considering the circumstance of course. I'll have the spaghetti please, if I may? Thank you. I'll say one thing for our Minister. Terrifically bright he may not be, but he is always open to suggestions. Is that pink stuff blancmange? I'll take the—jam roly-poly. Many thanks. You not eating?
Max No.
Leppard You ought to. We've a long night ahead of us in our different ways. Shall we sit? How long do you think before you can come up with a target?
Max Target?
Leppard Just a figure of speech.
Max I don't know.

Leppard This spaghetti is tinned. I know the Minister would very much appreciate some sort of feasibility study on his desk first thing tomorrow morning. But do finish your coffee first—sure you won't have anything to eat? Not hungry?

Max I consider that what you did was just about the greatest act of treachery that I can conceivably imagine.

Leppard That's putting it rather strongly, Max.

Max ORSONE was about pure scientific research. It was a chance to do things in a controlled gravity-free environment that we couldn't do down here. It was this country's greatest scientific opportunity for decades—and you sold all that down the river to the Americans so that they could put one over on the Warsaw Pact. It sickens me, Leppard.

Leppard Look at it realistically, Max. What was the point in having this wonderful piece of technology stuck down here on earth? We had to get it up somehow and the Americans were our only way of doing that. What did you want me to do? Play the foolish virgin? Blush and say "No thank you" very politely? There was too much at stake for us to do that, Max. Too much invested. It was a calculated risk that just happened to go wrong. Bad luck that's all. If this ridiculous accident hadn't happened nobody would have been any the wiser.

Max You've betrayed me personally.

Leppard Personally?

Max ORSONE was my project.

Leppard If I were a lesser man I'd suspect megalomania, Max. It was a team effort—our effort.

Max You're not one of us. Not a scientist. You never were. You're a political time-server. A Judas.

Leppard I'm sorry you feel like that, Max. Perhaps you should have come out of your ivory tower for a few days and tried to do my job. You talk to the politicians and argue with the Treasury. You smile all day long because you're afraid to stop smiling in case they take the money away. You'd soon learn.

Max You're breaking my heart.

Leppard And you're being unreasonable.

Max I'm being ... Do you know the kind of damage that those things could cause if they should happen to detonate when ORSONE comes down? .

Leppard Don't be childish, Max. Of course I do.

Max Tell me.

Leppard What.

Max Tell me.

Leppard Two megatons? It would take out an area of about two square miles if it were an air burst—five miles if it were a ground burst.

Max Take out?

Leppard It would destroy nearly all the buildings in that area of course, all animal and vegetable life. Re-occupation would be hazardous for at least twenty-five years.

Max And you can sit there and eat spaghetti.

Leppard I'm a realist, Max. These things happen. And once we know the precise area it will of course be thoroughly evacuated. Which is where I came in I think. You'd better get to work, Max. Time is of the essence, as our Minister would say—never been one to avoid the cliché. (*Quick pause*) Oh, Max. I'd like you to work very closely with this Thain woman on the public-image angle. Get together with her, will you? I can't tell you how pleased the Minister and I are that you agreed to soften the blow, as it were . . .

Max leaves the canteen restaurant and moves downstage

(*Going to the service counter*) I think I'd like to complain about this spaghetti . . .

The Lights cross fade to Max

Max Scene Four. Laboratory.

The Lights come up on the laboratory; a rather ramshackle place littered with print-outs etc. Max stands apart watching them working out calculations, consulting together, and so on

Odd thing to call it a laboratory. There's this wonderful public image of the new high-tec socieity that's all gleaming white surfaces, computers that talk, VDU screens everywhere. That's what the public sees. That is what men like Leppard want them to see. But most of the work—the crucial work ORSONE—was done on scraps of paper in a rented Portakabin in the car park at Headquarters, because the real work is done up here; the rest is just window-dressing . . .

Max enters the scene. Margaret, a pleasant, homely woman in her forties, puts down her pen and moves to him. Everyone stops work

Margaret Max.

Max You've heard then.

Margaret One of Leppard's minions phoned us all and got us in.

Max Have we got all the data we need?

Margaret A courier brought it all over from the computer.

Max Then we'd better get to work. They want a result by morning.

All go back to work except Margaret who takes Max aside

Margaret It is true then?

Max About it coming down. Of course.

Margaret About the other thing.

Max You heard?

Margaret Rumours.

Max They're all true, Margaret. That's if you listen to the same rumours as I do.

Margaret The bastards.

Max Leppard says it is the price we paid. Note the personal pronoun.

Margaret I feel . . .

Max I know. I know.

Margaret Ten years for this . . .

Max Ten? Ever since I was an undergraduate at Cambridge I dreamed of something like ORSONE and in those days that really was talking science fiction. Did I tell you my professor nearly had me taken away in a strait-jacket when I told him about my ambitions?

Margaret Resign.

Max I can't. Not yet. I'd be letting myself down.

Margaret Disassociate yourself then. You can't be seen to endorse what they've done when the news breaks.

Max I won't be. Don't worry.

Margaret What me, worry? Where's your pencil?

Max Right. Come on then, brains of Britain—one last calculation and then we can all go home. By the way did I ever tell you what the doctor said to the mathematician who complained of constipation . . . ?

The Lights fade to a spot on Max

An Englishman to the last—facing Armageddon with a joke on his stiff upper lip. By morning we had a result and by then the jokes didn't seem very funny anymore. Scene Five. Meeting.

The Lights were up on the meeting as before, with the Minister, Leppard, Amanda and Coley seated at the table. Max walks into the scene clutching papers

Minister Ah. Housden. It's all right, we haven't been waiting long. I was just saying to the others, the Prime Minister is most grateful for all the effort you're putting in on this crisis.

Max says nothing

Leppard Thank you, Minister. Very kind and much appreciated.
Minister Well there's no point in pussyfooting around; we're here for one thing and one thing only. Dr Housden?
Leppard Max?

No response from Max

"Your face is a book where men may read strange matters."

The Minister looks puzzled

Macbeth, Minister.
Minister Well?
Max I don't know how much you know about the control of satellites or vehicles in space but essentially what we can do with ORSONE is of a very limited capacity, largely because of its size. It does have retro-rockets so we are able to manoeuvre it within certain, very limited, parameters. We can fire these motors from the Control Centre and, in fact, they should have been fired the moment ORSONE's orbit began to decay. This would have pushed it out into a higher orbit. Out of harm's way for about two and a half thousand years—however that is what some people would call a spilt-milk situation. We can still fire those motors as ORSONE comes down and should we do so, we can forecast, with perhaps ninety per cent accuracy that it will make its point of impact at a location on—or somewhere near— Kodiak Island off the Alaska Peninsula. There's enough fuel on board for that.
Minister Alaska that's . . . ?

Coley The United States of America, Minister. It's near the Arctic Circle.

Leppard And—if we don't fire the motors?

Max England. (*He begins to laugh*)

Minister I don't consider that amusing.

Max What if I tell you that the point of impact in England would be a village called World's End?

Minister I still fail to see the joke. Where is this village?

Max (*still laughing*) Near Newbury.

Minister I think Dr Housden needs some sleep.

Max World's End.

Minister Well—I think we must thank Dr Housden and his colleagues for their dedicated labour in very difficult circumstances. And ... turn to you, Mr Coley.

Coley You mean you want to fire the motor?

Leppard If we're given the choice between the relatively unpopulated Arctic Circle and a high density population area in Berkshire. Well, I hardly think there is a choice do you?

Coley I'll have to consult with my superiors first.

Leppard And I've no doubt the Prime Minister will be talking to your President at the first opportunity.

Minister Naturally. Would it be indiscreet to point out that the devices are yours, so to speak. The ball seems to be in your court.

Coley The fact had not escaped me and I am sure our people would take that into account. If you'll excuse me.

Coley leaves the meeting rapidly

Minister Well, in point of fact I think things are turning out rather well. Quite a relief.

Leppard They certainly could be a lot worse, Minister.

Minister A sort of ... what would you call it—poetic justice?

Leppard Apt phrase.

Minister I think we may have got off rather lightly. The PM's going to be pleased. I may even get a glass of sherry out of it.

Leppard and the Minister leave the meeting laughing

Amanda World's End—you were joking?

Max You think I would joke about something like that?

Amanda You seemed to find it amusing enough.

Max I'm tired. I got hysterical.

Amanda We've got to talk.

Max About what?

Amanda About your interview. Now we've got the facts they'll want us to go ahead as soon as the news is announced.

Max To what end?

Amanda They're trying to save face. Despite all the evidence to the contrary they don't want to look like complete idiots.

Max They? You don't consider yourself one of them, Miss Thain?

Amanda I don't share their cynicism. Like you, I think that what they've done is appalling. I just think its best to present it in such a way as to alarm as few people as possible.

Max You're in the wrong job.

Amanda So are you—you should have stayed at Cambridge pottering about in academic research, building a reputation for eccentricity. You're not cut out for all this business. Its too high-powered for you.

Max That is rather a sweeping character judgement.

Amanda Not really—I wanted to be a philosopher. Look at me now.

Max What can I say in this interview?

Amanda Anything you like within reasons. Now that it's going to fall on the villain of the piece—as it were—it doesn't honestly make a lot of difference. Just watch what you say about HM Government and blind them with science. You should be good at that.

Max And my feelings on putting those things on board in the first place?

Amanda Stress the "biter bit" angle. Hoist them with their own petard. You could turn the whole thing to this country's advantage as well as appeasing your own outraged feelings.

Max Miss Thain. You have no moral standards. You'd have made a terrible philosopher.

Fade to spot on Max

I though I might be able to learn to live with it—not forgive them for what they'd done; not by any means—but Alaska— who really bothers about Alaska—except Alaskans—and they're aren't too many of them in the Arctic Tundra. I reasoned to myself—even if the things did go off it should be no worse than the average atmospheric nuclear test. I should have known better. Scene Six. American Embassy, Grosvenor Square. Imagination this one . . .

The Lights come up on Coley, Leppard, the Minister and the American Ambassadress, and two experts from Washington—one a high-ranking General, the other Cameron

Minister This is very bad news—very bad news indeed, Mr Ambassador.

Leppard Madam Ambassadress—Minister.

Minister The PM is going to throw a wobbly over this one. Are you sure of it?

Ambassadress The news has been confirmed from Washington I'm afraid—Mr Cameron here has flown over from the State Department in order to explain things more clearly to you. Mr Cameron?

Cameron Thank you, Madam Ambassadress. At this point we find ourselves in pretty much a no-win situation as far as this particular can of worms is concerned. The on-going knock-on effect from this situation will inevitably result in some form of domino effect as the geo-political situation—already in a de-neutralized condition as a result of a situational altering of perspectives in a no-go inter-contintental mode, in consequence of which we find ourselves in a no-go crisis situation situation.

Ambassadress Thank you Mr Cameron—do you have anything to add to that, General?

General No, no . . . I think Mr Cameron has put the situation very nicely. The position, ladies and gentlemen, is that we cannot risk another Kamchatka syndrome—even if its possibility is an outside one. If that were to occur we could find ourselves in a whole different ball game strategy-wise.

Ambassadress Thank you, General—that makes it very clear I think.

Minister I haven't a clue what anyone's talking about.

Leppard What our friends are saying, Minister, is this. As Housden pointed out there is a ninety per cent chance that ORSONE is going to come down on American territory near the Arctic Circle.

Coley Which would not be a problem.

Cameron Well put, Gerry.

Coley Thanks.

Leppard There is, however, a ten per cent possibility that it would not come down there. If, for example, the motors refused to cut out on order—or if we made a miscalculation—no matter how small—the regrettable fact is that—if that were to be the case—the next most likely area for landing would be sensitive to say the least——

General Sensitive! The whole damned can of worms could blow up. We'd have worms all over our face!

Ambassadress Well said, General. The problem, gentlemen, is that were ORSONE to miss its predicted drop-out point there is a ten per cent chance that it could land on Russian soil on or near the Kamchatka peninsular . . .

General And if you know what hot potatoes the Reds keep on Kamchatka you wouldn't want to get your fingers burned.

Ambassadress It is one of their most sensitive and secret military areas and they are very protective of it.

General They shot down that Korean Jumbo just for getting near it—if we put down any vehicle there you'd go very close to a reprisal situation. I need hardly remind you of the consequences if any nuclear activity were to be directed at them.

Ambassadress I'm afraid that my Government—and the President in particular—could not countenance such a possibility. It could well lead to conflagration on a global scale.

Minister You're telling us that we can't fire ORSONE's motors?

Cameron The State Department consider that the random, non-controllable risk factors are—at this point of time—too great.

Minister What's he saying?

Leppard It's too big a risk.

Minister It's a ten per cent risk.

General Too high, Minister, in our opinion.

Minister But they're your bloody nuclear weapons!

Ambassadress We fully appreciate the anomaly of the situation. And we do realize your dilemma.

Minister You're effectively asking me to drop your nuclear weapons on my own country because you're too scared to take a risk?

General I could point out, Minister, that you and your Government agreed to the devices being put on board in the first place.

Minister As a return favour. And we thought they were for our
protection—not destruction.

Cameron You were aware you were in a walking-the-tightrope
situation.

General And you were very pleased to accept the protection that
was offered.

Minister You're supposed to be our bloody allies.

Ambassadress We will of course do all we can to help if the
ultimate scenario occurs. Economic aid would be forthcoming
as would any moral support we can offer.

Minister What if we were to fire the motors in any case?

General There is no question of our allowing you to do that.

Minister Allowing?

General Certain precautionary measures have already been taken.
You will find I think that your telemetric links with ORSONE
are already non-operative.

Leppard You're jamming our radio links?

General And our personnel are by now in full control of your
Control Centre.

Ambassadress It's a regrettable necessity—we are really very
sorry.

Cameron There are of course a great many on-going operational
precautionary scenarios that you can operate in such a no-
choice situation as this.

Minister What the bloody hell does that mean?

Leppard I think it means we should start ducking . . .

The Lights fade to a spot on Max, seated at a table

Max And, like a lamb to the slaughter, there I was putting on an
acceptable human face on what was fundamentally unaccep-
table. Scene Seven. TV Studio.

*An Interviewer joins Max and sits at the table as the Lights come up
on the TV studio where Technicians, a Floor Manager, etc. and
Amanda, stand watching a monitor screen*

Interviewer In conclusion, Dr Housden, how do you feel at what
was to be purely a scientific project being perverted into an
extension of the arms race?

Max I think I've got to take issue with the word perverted. Bear in
mind that the original intention of our American friends in

putting these devices on ORSONE was to see how such equipment would behave in gravity-free environments for prolonged periods of time.

Interviewer Do you really believe that was their prime motive?

Max I do—yes. And don't forget that nobody could have anticipated or predicted this grotesque accident. We should all be grateful that the consequences will not be anywhere as serious as they might have been.

Interviewer Thank you, Dr Housden.

The spot fades on the Interviewer and Max. The news continues on the monitor set. Max crosses to Amanda

Max Did you ever feel that you'd just sold everything you believed in down the river?

Amanda You'll recover.

Max Oh yes. I'm safe enough now.

Attention is focused on the monitor

Newscaster's voice But it appears there has been a new development in the ORSONE story. We go over live to Whitehall.

The following sequence between the Journalists and the Minister may be recorded

Journalist 1 Have you any comments on this new development, Minister?

Minister They'll be a statement later on.

Journalist 2 Is it true that the Americans won't let it come down in Alaska?

Minister Regrettably—yes.

Journalist 3 What response have you made to that?

Minister I've expressed the Government's disappointment.

Journalist 4 What about the alternative site, Minister?

Minister No comment.

Journalist 1 Is it in this country?

Minister This will be dealt with later on. All I can say is that in co-operation with our American allies we have encountered difficulties in the resolution of the ORSONE project which necessitates a switch in the ultimate drop-out point.

Journalist 1 What about the nuclear devices, Minister?

Minister No comment. Excuse me . . .

Max They've betrayed us.
Amanda I'm sorry.
Max It's World's End then ... I wish I could remember why I
thought that funny.

The Lights fade to a spot on Max

Naturally, resignation is the only decent course in such circumstances. Nobody in my position with any semblance of moral
conviction could even contemplate staying on. I stayed on. I
thought I could help soften the blow somehow when it came.
Scene Eight. Church Hall. World's End.

*The Lights cross fade to a church hall crowded with leading villagers,
sitting on benches etc. The Minister, Leppard and Max have been
conducting some sort of enquiry session*

Minister In conclusion I can only assure you that the Government, utilizing the full resources of the public services and the
military will begin evacuation of the whole area within a twenty
mile radius, commencing tomorrow. I would just remind you
that there is no need to panic, since we have plenty of time
before—the deadline expires. That is the position as it now
stands and I can assure you categorically that everything is very
much under control.
Max Except of course, the one thing that matters.

A man in the audience rises

Man When you said twenty mile radius I take it you meant
diameter?
Leppard The Minister meant radius.
Man I see.
Minister Merely as a precautionary measure naturally. There is no
guarantee that damage will be on anything like that scale.
Leppard There is no guarantee even of a nuclear contingency.
Max No need to sound disappointed ...
Woman (*rising*) I take it we are to be compensated?
Minister In full. And I wish to stress in full.
Man And when—if the worst happens—shall we be able to move
back?
Minister Dr Leppard—perhaps you could ...

Leppard Such a calculation is extraordinarily difficult to make in view of the unknown factors. One could hazard.

Max Never.

Minister Dr Housden.

Max That's it. Never. Not in your lifetimes anyway—probably not in those of your children.

A murmur begins

Minister Now, there seems little point in considering what are at worst, rather remote possibilities at this juncture.

Man What about my turkeys?

Minister The gentleman at the back.

Man I've got a hundred thousand turkeys on my farm. I retired early and put all my savings in this. If they're roasted in this thing it'll take me years to build up my stock again.

Minister I have said that everybody will be compensated.

Man But listen here. Who's going to cough up the money for all this compensation. It's going to take millions!

Minister We are in the process of working out compensation agreements with our American allies. We have every reason to believe that it will be a generous agreement.

Max They've agreed to open another Kentucky Fried Chicken in Newbury. You'll have a ready-made market. Exchange after all, is no robbery . . .

Leppard Dr Housden is not being entirely serious.

Mrs Judd stands up. She is an august woman in her sixties

Mrs Judd What about the religious aspect of all this?

Minister I beg your pardon?

Mrs Judd Where does God stand in all this?

Minister I don't feel qualified to answer that question.

Max Uncharacteristic modesty.

Mrs Judd You don't, for example, see these events as a punishment sent from God to chastise us for our pride and vainglory in seeking to take upon ourselves the godlike powers of creation and destruction?

Minister That doesn't form part of the Government's thinking at the moment, certainly.

Mrs Judd Then might I recommend the Book of Revelations to you? You'll find it most enlightening.

Minister Yes. Thank you.
Mrs Judd May I add that I certainly shall not be voting for you next time?

She sits down to ragged applause. She stands up again

Thank you.

A Young Woman stands up

Young Woman I wonder if the scientists on the platform would be willing to make some sort of statement about how they view their responsibilities in this matter. Because it seems to me that it is they who have fundamentally betrayed us. It is they who have countenanced and abetted the creation of this monstrosity. They who have dedicated their lives and their work to something evil and anti-human. They who have given the politicians—who haven't even the sense of children—the most dangerous and destructive toys that imagination can conceive of.

Applause and agreement

Minister Dr Housden?
Max I can't answer that.

Jeers

I can't answer that because I agree with everything that you've said.
Leppard Max——
Max From whatever misguided hopes and motives, I have helped the create this deplorable catastrophe. I can't even claim naïvety because I've seen ideas and concepts that started out in glorious optimism and hope being taken over by people who couldn't, or wouldn't, see their true possibilities; who wanted to gain a few easy points and scramble further up the ladder. I've seen all that happen before. I thought that this time it would be different. I was wrong.

The Lights cross fade to a spot on Max in the bar

It seems so easy to admit culpability and responsibility. After all, there was no danger to human life; just a lot of property being destroyed, and property can be replaced. All it meant was a bit of discomfort, a certain amount of reorganization. My conscience felt relatively clear; perhaps there was even a touch of pleasure in the self-righteousness I felt. Then this happened. Scene Nine. Church. World's End.

The Lights cross fade to the church. Benches are arranged as pews; perhaps a suggestion of stained glass in the lighting. Women from the village sit around in what has evidently been a long occupation. A Police Superintendent is present with a few other officers, also the Minister and Leppard and a Bishop and the local vicar, the Reverend Blishen

Minister And you categorically refuse to move?

Young Woman Categorically, allegorically, metaphorically—any way you like. We refuse.

Superintent I trust you realize what a serious matter this is?

Young Woman Possibly more than you do.

Minister Superintendent? The rest of the area has been evacuated?

Superintendent Two days ago, sir.

Leppard And they still refuse to go.

Superintendent They claim to be making some sort of statement. Muddle-headed, if you ask me.

Minister What's the legal position on this one?

Superintendent Strictly   speaking,   they're   trespassing,   but obviously there are complications.

Minister I don't like complications.

Bishop I think the Superintendent is saying that the question of trespassing in a House of God is, necessarily, a tricky one.

Minister Are you prepared to bring charges?

Bishop I should have to refer to a higher authority.

The Minister looks at him

I mean Canterbury. But I believe the Archbishop's view would be the same as my own.

Leppard Which is?

Bishop That these ladies—misguided though they may be—are treating this building as a place of—for want of a better word— sanctuary. In such a position I would be very loath to evict them.

Superintendent It won't be much of a sanctuary in twelve hours' time.

Bishop Nevertheless, it would seem to outside observers that the

Church was withdrawing its comfort and protection at a time when it was most needed.

Minister Then we shall have to evoke the Emergency Powers Act.

Bishop That is your decision.

Minister Muster your men, Superintendent.

Young Woman Are you going to throw us out?

Minister I'm having you removed under the Emergency Powers Act for your own safety. We can't allow any unnecessary loss of life.

Young Woman Our lives are our concern. We don't wish to be evacuated.

Minister What you wish has very little to do with it.

Young Woman All we wish to do is to face up to the implications of what you and your kind have created. That's a democratic right. If we happen to die in the process then that is also our democratic right.

Minister Spurious arguments. If I don't have you removed to safety I am—I am . . .

Leppard Abrogating.

Minister Abrogating the Government's responsibilities.

Young Woman You can talk about responsibilities? Listen, I'll argue on your level since it's the only level you seem to understand. You have us forcibly removed and do you know what all those camera crews and photographers out there are going to do? They're going to have you for breakfast and laugh while they're doing it. You prepared to risk that?

The Minister pauses

Minister Leppard. Do you think she's right?

Leppard There is a regrettable logic in what she says, certainly. We—you—are in what our American friends would christen a "no-win situation". A horrible but apt phrase. Might I suggest that the Reverend——

Blishen Blishen.

Leppard Yes. You know most of these women personally. Perhaps word from you might tip the scales.

Blishen I've tried already.

Minister Try again.

Blishen Bishop?

Bishop Try again.

The Minister and Leppard leave the Church

Blishen Ladies, I beg you to reconsider your position.

Young Woman Wasting your time.

Blishen But this is a futile sacrifice. Quite futile. This is not to say that we—the Church—do not recognize your bravery, your idealism—but the situation is totally irreversible. You'll achieve nothing.

Bishop And enough is enough.

Young Woman Meaning?

Blishen That you've surely made your point. That you can stop now.

Young Woman While that thing is still up there?

Bishop Nothing is going to change that.

Young Woman Then we can't stop either, can we?

Bishop Surely we can look upon the whole affair as a mistake? A regrettable mistake but a mistake nonetheless.

Young Woman Human folly?

Bishop Exactly.

Young Women Not evil but folly.

Bishop God has given us free will and we have chosen to create such things. Whether that is evil or foolishness or both isn't a matter that we can decide here. The fact is that such devices exist and your deaths will not stop them existing.

Blishen And insofar as these weapons have kept a kind of peace, albeit through fear, can we not say that they have been of some value?

Young Woman You refuse to condemn these abominations as evil?

Bishop That is not the Church's view at the present moment.

Young Woman Then there's really nothing more to say, is there?

Blishen It seems not.

Bishop It saddens me to see the waste.

Blishen I think, though, my Lord, that very few of them are believers.

Bishop Is that meant to reassure me?

Mrs Judd enters the Church

Mrs Judd Bishops aren't meant to need reassurance.

Blishen This is Mrs Judd, my Lord. One of my regular congregation.

Mrs Judd I'm so heartened to see that you gentlemen have joined the rest of us. Your presence will be a great comfort.

Blishen You're staying here?

Mrs Judd Of course. You're not?

Bishop It's our view that the Reverend Blishen's talents will be of greater use elsewhere.

Mrs Judd A nice way of sticking your head in the sand.

Bishop Mrs Judd?

Mrs Judd That's the way I see it. Is that not the way you see it?

Bishop Not entirely.

Mrs Judd We all helped to put those things up there in the sense that we gave those people the power to do so and didn't stop them when we could. If we've got anything about us we'd better face up to the consequences of that or we're sticking our heads in the sand. That's why I'm here.

An embarrassed pause

Blish Might I suggest we leave, my Lord? There isn't that much time.

A moment between the Bishop and Mrs Judd. Then Blishen and the Bishop leave

Young Woman We weren't expecting you.

Mrs Judd Idealism is not the sole preserve of the young, despite what the newspapers tell us. In any case, I'd rather go with a bang than a whimper.

Young Woman I think we can guarantee that.

Mrs Judd Good. Good.

Max enters the church

Young Woman You're not welcome here.

Max I haven't come to persuade you to leave.

Third Woman That makes no difference.

Mrs Judd Aren't you one of these scientists?

Max I didn't invent it to destroy.

First Woman But that's what it's going to do.

Max You haven't got the monopoly on idealism. Can't you imagine that what made me dedicate fifteen years or more of my life to this project was something very similar to what you're feeling now? Things have gone wrong that's all. Events have overtaken me.

Second Woman I saw you on television. Justifying what you'd
  done and what was going to happen. Calling them our "Ameri-
  can friends" and saying everything was going to be all right.
Max That was a mistake. I didn't know.
Second Woman Know what?
Max That it was going to hit here.
Mrs Judd You still haven't grasped it, have you—none of you
  have. It doesn't matter where it's going to hit—it's the fact that
  these things are up there at all and that there's a chance that they
  are going to come down anywhere that's terrifying—whether it's
  Alaska or here. Haven't you grasped that yet?
Max I came here to make my peace.
First Woman Too late. You weren't thinking of staying by any
  chance?
Max I don't know.
First Woman No way. We're not condoning your martyrdom.
  You don't get off the hook that easily.
Mrs Judd I think you'd better go.
Max If it's any help it'll come down at just about four o'clock
  tomorrow morning. If any of you change your mind you'll be
  safe from any risk if you leave up to an hour before and get
  more than twenty miles away.
Second Woman We won't be changing our minds.

The Lights cross fade to spot on Max seated at a table in the bar

Max It was the idea that I wanted to be a martyr too that hurt—
  probably because it was true. They all stayed.

*The Lights cross fade to the church. It is the early hours of the
morning. The church clock chimes four. The Lights cross fade to
Max as before*

When a one megaton device explodes everything within two
miles of the explosion is completely destroyed. The blast creates
a crater one thousand feet in diameter and two hundred feet
deep. Human beings close to the point of explosion are vapour-
ized by the heat of the fireball and everyone else in the area is
killed by incineration or falling buildings. Most buildings within
a radius of three to five miles catch fire because of heat from the
fireball and in some cases coalesce into one huge fire storm,
sucking air into its centre at speeds of up to three hundred miles

an hour; Temperatures can exceed a thousand degrees centigrade at the centre of the fire storm. Most people in that area would be killed by heat, fire, asphyxiation. In a ground-burst radio active fall-out can fall on an area up to two hundred and fifty miles from point of explosion causing radiation sickness and tens of thousands of deaths and casualties. I could describe the symptoms of radiations sickness but I leave that to your imagination.

The Lights come up on the bar. Max, seated at the table, is by now drunk. The life of the bar goes on around him as normal. Margaret enters, looks around and sees him

Margaret Max.

He looks up

You're surely not drunk?
Max As a skunk, Margaret. Have one?
Margaret Why on earth did you come here?
Max Because I wanted to get drunk. A pub seemed — logical.
Margaret But nobody ever comes here.
Max That's why I came here. I wanted to think.
Margaret What about?
Max Of "purposes mistook, fall'n on th' inventors' heads"?
Margaret What?
Max Are you sure you're not drinking?
Margaret We go through this routine every time you have to fly. Pull yourself together, Max. I've got your luggage waiting in a taxi outside.
Max Taxi?
Margaret To take you to the airport. You know? Big silver bird in sky?
Max Zoom.
Margaret That's it. You can nurture your hangover in Florida.
Max Where the orange juice comes from.
Margaret And where little men send up big shuttle to the stars.

Max's face straightens

Max Yes.
Margaret And the day after tomorrow the little men are going to

put a special present on board, aren't they? A special little present that we've made.

Max ORSONE.

Margaret That's right.

A pause

Max It started like this.

The Lights fade to Black-out

FURNITURE AND PROPERTY LIST

On stage: Bar counter. *On it:* glasses, drink etc. *Under it (pre-set for changes of scenes):* plate of spaghetti, bowl of pink blanc-mange, dish of jam roly-poly, cups, saucers, tray, cutlery etc., print-outs, pens, laboratory equipment etc., papers for **(Max)**

Tables
Chairs
Benches
Telephone

LIGHTING PLOT

Practical fittings required: flashing lights, TV screens (monitor, VDU, etc.), space invaders or pinball machine (optional).

Cue 14	**Max:** ". . . a terrible philosopher." *Cross fade to spot on* **Max**	(Page 18)
Cue 15	**Max:** "Imagination this one . . ." *Cross fade to interior effect on Embassy area*	(Page 19)
Cue 16	**Leppard:** "I think it means we should start ducking . . ." *Cross fade to spot on* **Max**	(Page 21)
Cue 17	**Max:** "Scene Seven. TV Studio." *Bring up lighting on TV studio with TV effect from monitor screen*	(Page 21)
Cue 18	**Interviewer:** "Thank you, Dr Housden." *Fade spot*	(Page 23)
Cue 19	**Max:** ". . . why I thought that funny." *Cross fade to spot on* **Max**	(Page 23)
Cue 20	**Max:** "Church Hall. World's End." *Cross fade to interior effect on church hall*	(Page 23)
Cue 21	**Max:** "I was wrong." *Cross fade to spot on* **Max**	(Page 25)
Cue 22	**Max:** "Church. World's End." *Cross fade to church with stained-glass effect*	(Page 26)
Cue 23	**Second Woman:** "We won't be changing our minds." *Cross fade to spot on* **Max**	(Page 30)
Cue 24	**Max:** "They all stayed." *Cross fade to church to give easily morning effect*	(Page 30)
Cue 25	Clock chimes four *Cross fade to spot on* **Max**	(Page 30)
Cue 26	**Max:** ". . . to your imagination." *Cross fade to interior effect on bar*	(Page 31)
Cue 27	**Max:** "It started like this." *Fade to Black-out*	(Page 32)

EFFECTS PLOT

Cue 1   **Max:** "It started like this . . ."   (Page 1)
         Buzzers etc.

Cue 2   **Operator 2:** "Six point two per cent."   (Page 2)
         Phone

Cue 3   Lights come up on the entrance hall   (Page 3)
         Doorbell, knocking on front door

Cue 4   The Lights cross fade to the church   (Page 30) .
         Church clock strikes four

MADE AND PRINTED IN GREAT BRITAIN BY
LATIMER TREND & COMPANY LTD, PLYMOUTH
MADE IN ENGLAND